US Immigration Exam Study Guide in English and Tagalog

Mike Swedenberg

Contact me at: Mike@Swedenberg.com

Twitter: @USAcitizenship

US Citizenship Test Study Guide in English and Tagalog

Study Guide
100 Questions and Answers to the US Immigration Test
in English and Tagalog

Gabay sa Pag-aaral ng US Citizenship Test sa Ingles
lahat ng Unidos-aral Gabay
100 Tanong at Sagot sa Tagalog at Ingles

Lahat ng Karapatan Ginawa sa USA

A unique product, professionally developed and annotated.
**Lists all current Senators, Congressmen,
Governors and State Capitols plus Legal Advice**

Ang isang natatanging produkto, propesyonal na binuo at
itinala.
**Naglilista ng lahat ng kasalukuyang mga Senators,
Congressmen, Governors at Estado Capitols**

Bi Lingual Languages available:
Spanish, English only, Polish, Albanian, French, Portuguese, Russian,
Korean, Chinese, Vietnamese and Tagalog.

DEDICATION

To those wishing to become an American Citizen.

The U.S. Citizenship Services (USCIS) administers a verbal test to all immigrants applying for citizenship. This study guide tutors Tagalog (Philippine) speaking immigrants for the USCIS verbal citizenship test. The questions have been selected from questions used on past exams by the USCIS.

Ang US Citizenship Serbisyo (USCIS) ay nangangasiwa ng pandiwang pagsubok sa lahat ng mga imigrante na-aplay para sa pagkamamamayan. Ito gabay ng pag-aaral tutors Tagalog (Philippine) nagsasalita ng mga imigrante para sa USCIS pandiwang pagkamamamayan ng pagsubok. Ang mga katanungan ay pinili mula sa mga katanungan na ginamit sa nakaraang pagsusulit ng USCIS.

Studying these questions does not guarantee obtaining citizenship to the United States.
Pag-aaral sa mga tanong na ito ay hindi ginagarantiya ang pagkuha ng pagkamamamayan sa Estados Unidos.

CONTENTS

"I pledge allegiance to the flag of the United States of America, and to the republic for which it stands, one nation under God, indivisible, with liberty and justice for all."

ACKNOWLEDGMENTS

We are grateful for the cooperation of the U.S. Citizenship Services (USCIS) in the preparation of this study guide

Good luck on the test.

INTRODUCTION

The 100 sample questions and answers for the US Immigration test are listed below. The test is an oral exam in which the USCIS Officer will ask the applicant up to 10 of the 100 questions. An applicant must answer six out of ten questions correctly to pass the civics portion of the test.

On the naturalization test, some answers may change because of elections or appointments. As you study for the test, make sure that you know the most current members of Congress, Senate, Speaker of the House and Governor of your state and district.

This publication is the only study guide that provides this information and updates it throughout the year.

We also provide you with the Sample Written Questions which all applicants must know how to write in English.

A guide to U.S. State Postal Abbreviations has been added for the List of Senators

ADVICE

from the Immigration Law offices of

KURCZABA LAW OFFICES P.C.

6219 N. Milwaukee - Chicago, IL 60646

10661 S. Roberts Rd., Palos Hills, IL 60465

(773) 774-0000

www.kurczabalaw.com

BECOMING A CITIZEN

The day of your interview, you will be asked to appear at a specific date and time at the

Immigration Office. For interviews in Chicago, our interview will take place at:

101 W. Ida B. Wells (formerly Congress Parkway), 3rd Floor

Chicago

Bring to the interview:

Interview notice

Passports – all your passports, current and expired

Permanent Resident Card (green card)

Driver's License/ ID

Income Tax Returns – bring your last 5 years of tax returns (may be asked)

Alimony/Child Support – (if required to pay) – bring proof of payment Check In:

Arrive 30 minutes before your scheduled interview

Check in with the receptionist (in Chicago - on the 3rd floor) – they will give you a number

You will be called by number

Interview:

When called, you will enter the officer's room, and:

Oath – swear that you will tell the truth.

Fingerprint /identification– the officer will take your photograph (using a digital camera) and ask you to place your left and right index finger on a little black box on their desk.

Administer the following test

1.TEST

Questions – 100 possible Questions – as listed in this book

You will be given 10 questions - 2 from each section,

You must have 6 correct. As soon as you have 6 correct – you pass and the question portion of the test ends.

Reading- you will be asked to read a question out loud to the officer (usually shown on an iPad)

Writing – you will be asked to write a sentence on the same iPad which is dictated to you. (in Chicago – this is often the answer to the question you just read)

2.APPLICATION

You will be asked questions from the Citizenship Application (form N400).

Biographical information

Name (your full name – first, middle last) as shown on your birth certificate

Any other names used – including your maiden (before marriage) name

Address, telephone,

Your marital status

Spouse's name, date of birth, date of marriage, immigration status (if out of status – you may state this, you may also state that you are applying for permanent residency for them). If your spouse is a US Citizen already, you may bring a copy of their Naturalization Certificate

Children – their names, dates of birth, locations of birth, current address (often city is sufficient)

Details on employment, residency

Travel History – when is the last time you left the United States? Sometimes officers will ask you have you left the United States since filing your N-400 application? OR Have you ever been outside of the United States for 180 days or longer? You may check your travel history on the Customs and Border Protection Website at: https://i94.cbp.dhs.gov/I94/#/home

If you have been outside of the United States for longer than 180 days at any one time, be prepared to provide detailed information as to why you stayed outside of the country for so long. If for education reasons – provide proof of attending school, for job reasons – bring a letter from your employer, because of illness – bring proof of your seeking medical attention.

It is up to the Immigration Officer to determine whether your permanent place of residence is in the United States, and there was good reason for you to have to remain outside of the country for > 6 months. Officers will look to the exact reasons for your staying longer outside the country.

In the past 5 years, you must have spent at least > ½ of that time in the United States. This means out of 1,825 days; you must have spent > 913 days in the United States. If you have not – you do not qualify for naturalization.

Did you ever serve in the military? When? What branch?

How you received permanent residency?

If you obtained permanent residency through a spouse – are you still married to that spouse? Bring proof with you including joint filed tax returns, bank account statements, insurance statements, proof of residency. If you are divorced – bring your divorce decree (issued by a court) and be ready to explain why you were divorced.

If you obtained permanent residency through an employer – be prepared to give information about your sponsoring employer, the name of the owner, address and telephone of the company, and the occupation you were sponsored in for permanent residency. The officer may also ask if you had experience in that occupation before being sponsored, and where you were working to gain that experience.

Your eligibility for citizenship – most asked questions – see later questions for a full listing.

Did you ever claim to be a US Citizen?

The immigration service has been adopting a strict approach to this question. If you have ever stated that you were a citizen, you can expect to be denied and the Immigration Service to start proceedings against you to lose your permanent residence.

Did you ever vote or register to vote in an American election?

Did you ever discriminate against anyone?

Did you ever lie to immigration/ use false documents?

Do you owe any taxes?

Did you ever file taxes as a nonresident (after receiving your permanent residency)?

Do you have a title of nobility?

Were you ever a member of the military?

If so – was it mandatory? When did you serve? What was your title/rank?

Do you have any weapons training?

If so – what kind of weapons?

Are you a member of a terrorist or socialist organization?

If a male, did you live in the US between ages 18-26? Did you register for Selective Service?

Be prepared to provide proof of the registration which you can obtain by checking the Selective Service Administration at https://www.sss.gov/Home/Verification

Citizenship Issues

Are you ready to take the oath of allegiance?

Did you read and understand the oath? (copy in this book)

If the law requires, are you ready to sign up to the military and defend the United States?

If the law requires, are you ready to assist the government in a civilian capacity in a time of national emergency?

OATH

You will be asked if you are ready to take the Oath of Citizenship. You should be familiar with what the oath says, but do not have to memorize it. The oath generally says that you will be loyal to the United States and defend this country.

I hereby declare, on oath, that I absolutely and entirely renounce and abjure all allegiance and fidelity to any foreign prince, potentate, state, or sovereignty, of whom or which I have heretofore been a subject or citizen; that I will support and defend the Constitution and laws of the

United States of America against all enemies, foreign and domestic; that I will bear true faith and allegiance to the same; that I will bear arms on behalf of the United States when required by the law; that I will perform noncombatant service in the Armed Forces of the United States when required by the law; that I will perform work of national importance under civilian direction when required by the law; and that I take this obligation freely, without any mental reservation or purpose of evasion; so help me God."

TEST

1. 10 Questions (6 correct)

2. Read a Question Out Loud

3. Write a Sentence

 Three Tests for Citizenship

Most applicants for citizenship or naturalization as it is called, are

subject to THREE different "tests" when applying. It is important

that an individual understand that in applying for Citizenship their

entire immigration history is being reviewed and an Immigration

Officer is making a determination not only over whether an

applicant passes a test, but moreover, is reviewing the applicant's

entire immigration history.

The Citizenship process should be looked upon as a complex,

detailed demanding process, not just the completion of a form and

passing of a simple civics test. This is not a process that should be taken lightly.

Often persons get "free" help with benevolent charities completing applications during large scale meetings. However, an applicant can face severe consequences including the loss of their permanent residency and even removal from the United States if certain matters come to the attention of an Immigration Officer reviewing your application.

First and foremost are persons who have ever been arrested, detained, or even stopped by a Police Officer.   These individuals should ensure they seek the assistance of an attorney to review their criminal record before proceeding with the filing of an application for Citizenship.

Each Applicant for Citizenship undergoes three tests:

1. Test of Civics/History/Government, Reading & Writing

a. Civics/history test of 10 questions chosen out of a possible 100

b. Reading – applicants will be asked to read out loud a sample sentence from a fixed set of possible sentences

c. Writing – applicants will be asked to write a sentence dictated by an Immigration Officer.

2. Ability to Communicate in English

a. The Immigration Officer will review your application with you. Traditionally, this takes place after you pass your test. This portion can be difficult for those that do not speak English well.

b. The Immigration Officer will speak to you in English to determine if you generally can communicate.

3. Eligibility –a review of an Applicant's personal history

a. The Immigration Officer will review your entire immigration file and determine if you have the proper character to become a citizen. The Officer will literally have before them your entire immigration history including every form and piece of paper that you submitted to the Immigration Service. This includes your applications for immigration benefits before permanent residency.

i. The Officer will review how you obtained your green card or permanent residency.

1. If you received your permanent residency through marriage to a US Citizen, then the Immigration Officer will ask questions about your marriage. The Officer can question whether the marriage was legitimate.

2. If you received your permanent residency through a family member – the Immigration Officer will review your original application to make sure there were no improprieties when you applied.

3. If you received your permanent residency through an employer – the Immigration Officer can ask you questions about the employer and the employment relationship.

ii. The Officer will review your criminal background – checking if you were ever arrested/detained/stopped by a Police Officer at home or abroad.

1. For the Immigration Service- to be stopped, arrested, or detained means precisely that – any time a Police agency would take your fingerprints

a. Regardless of the eventual outcome of the case – or what you think it means to be arrested – you will be expected to admit to all times that you were arrested/stopped or detained by a Police agency.

i. Sometimes applicants believe that an arrest means serving time in jail. But the Immigration Service has a much broader interpretation – including anytime that a Police agency would take your fingerprints and record the information.

ii. The Immigration Service obtains criminal background information on individuals primarily from the FBI. The FBI retains this information forever, regardless of expungements, or local agencies clearing of a criminal history.

AMERICAN GOVERNMENT

PAMAHALAAN NG AMERIKA

Principles of American Democracy

Mga Prinsipyo ng Demokrasyang Amerikano

1. What is the supreme law of the land?

   The Constitution

1. Ano ang pinakamataas na batas ng bansa?

   ang Konstitusyon

2. What does the Constitution do?

   Sets up the government

   Defines the government

   Protects basic rights of Americans

2. Ano ang Ginagawa ng Konstitusyon?

   itinatatag ang pamahalaan

   binibigyan ng kahulugan ang pamahalaan

   nagpoprotekta sa mga basikong karapatan ng mga

   Amerikano

3. The idea of self-government is in the first three words of

   the Constitution. What are these words?

   We the People

3. Ang ideya ng sariling-pamamahala ay nasa unang tatlong salita ng Konstitusyon. Ano ang mga salitang ito?

    Tayong mga Tao

4. What is an amendment?

    A change to the Constitution.

    An addition to the Constitution.

4. Ano ang isang susog?

    isang pagbabago (sa Konstitusyon)

    bilang karagdagan (sa Konstitusyon)

5. What do we call the first ten amendments to the Constitution?

    The Bill of Rights

5. Ano ang tinatawag na unang sampung susog sa Kontistusyon?

    ang Batas sa mga Karapatan

6. What is one right or freedom from the First Amendment? (You need to know one answer)

    Speech

    Religion

    Assembly

    Press

    Petition the government

6. Ano ang isang karapatan o kalayaan mula sa Unang Susog?*

> pagsasalita

> relihiyon

> pagtitipon

> pamamahayag

> magpetisyon sa pamahalaan

7. How many amendments does the Constitution have?

> Twenty-seven (27)

7. Ilang susog mayroon ang Konstitusyon?

> dalawampu't-pito (27)

8. What did the Declaration of Independence do?

> Announced our independence (from Great Britain)

> Declared our independence (from Great Britain)

> Said that the United States is free (from Great Britain)

8. Ano ang ginagawa ng Deklarasyon ng Kalayaan?

> ipinahayag ang ating kalayaan (mula sa Great Britain)

> idineklara ang ating kalayaan (mula sa Great Britain)

> sinabi na ang Estados Unidos ay malaya (mula sa Great Britain)

9. What are two rights in the Declaration of Independence?

Life

Liberty

Pursuit of Happiness

9. Ano ang dalawang karapatan sa Deklarasyon sa Kalayaan?

buhay

kalayaan

la paghahangad ng kaligayahan

10. What is freedom of religion?

You can practice any religion, or not practice a religion.

10. Ano ang kalayaan sa relihiyon?

Maaari kang magpraktis ng anumang relihiyon, o hindi magpraktis ng relihiyon.

11. What is the economic system in the United States?*

capitalist economy

market economy

11. Ano ang sistema ng ekonomiya sa Estados Unidos?*

kapitalistang ekonomiya

ekonomiya ng pamiliha

12. What is the "rule of law"?

Everyone must follow the law

Leaders must obey the law.

Government must obey the law.

No one is above the law

12. Ano ang "pamamayani ng batas"?

Ang bawat isa ay dapat sumunod ng batas.

Ang mga lider ay dapat sumunod sa batas.

Ang pamahalaan ay dapat sumunod sa batas.

Walang hindi sakop ng batas.

System of Government

Sistema ng Pamahalaan

13. Name one branch or part of the government.*

    Congress

    Legislative

    President

    Executive

    The courts

    Judicial

13. Sabihin ang isang sangay o bahagi ng pamahalaan.*

    Kongreso

    pambatasan

    Pangulo

    ehekutibo

    mga korte

    panghukuman

14. What stops one branch of government from becoming too powerful?

Checks and balances

Separation of powers

14. Ano ang pumipigil sa isang sangay ng pamahalaan na maging masyadong makapangyarihan?

mga pagsusuri at pagbalanse

paghihiwalay ng mga kapangyarihan

15. Who is in charge of the executive branch?

The President

15. Sino ang namamahala sa sangay na ehekutibo?

ang Pangulo

16. Who makes federal laws?

Congress

Senate and House (of Representatives)

(U.S. or national) legislature

16. Sino ang gumagawa ng mga pederal na batas?

Kongreso

Senado at Kapulungan (ng mga Kinatawan)

(Estados Unidos o pambansang) lehislatura

17. What are the two parts of the U.S. Congress?*

 The Senate and House (of Representatives)

17. Ano ang dalawang bahagi ng Kongreso ng Estados Unidos?*

 the Senado at Kapulungan (ng mga Kinatawan)

18. How many U.S. Senators are there?

 One hundred (100)

18. Ilang Senador ng Estados Unidos ay mayroon?

 isang daan (100)

19. We elect a U.S. Senator for how many years?

 Six (6)

19. Inihahalal natin ang isang Senador ng Estados Unidos para sa ilang taon?

 anim (6)

20. Who is one of your state's U.S. Senators?*

<u>See list below</u>. Answers will vary. For District of Columbia residents and residents of U.S. territories, the answer is that D.C. (or the territory where the applicant lives) has no U.S. Senators.

20. Sino ang isa sa mga Senador ng inyong estado ngayon?*

Ang mga sagot ay magkakaiba. [Ang mga residente ng District of Columbia at mga residente ng mga teritoryo ng Estados Unidos ay dapat sumagot na ang D.C. (o ang teritoryo kung saan nakatira ang aplikante) ay walang mga Senador ng Estados Unidos.]

See back of the book and write your answer here:

---

* If you are 65 years old or older and have been a legal permanent resident of the United States for 20 or more years, you may study just the questions that have been marked with an asterisk.

* Kung ikaw ay 65 taong gulang o mas matanda at naging legal na permanenteng residente ng Estados Unidos ng 20 o higit na taon, maaari mong pag-aralan ang mga katanungan lamang na minarkahan ng asterisk.

21. The House of Representatives has how many voting members?

Four hundred thirty-five (435)

21. Ang Kapulungan ng mga Kinatawan ay may ilang bumobotong miyembro?

apat na raan tatlumpu't-lima (435)

22. We elect a U.S. Representative for how many years?.

Two (2)

22. Naghahalal tayo ng Kinatawan ng Estados Unidos para sa ilang taon?

dalawa (2)

23. Name your U.S. Representative..

Answers will vary. [Residents of territories with nonvoting Delegates or resident Commissioners may provide the name of that Delegate or Commissioner. Also acceptable is any statement that the territory has no (voting) Representatives in Congress.]

23. Sabihin kung sino ang inyong Kinatawan ng Estados Unidos.

Ang mga sagot ay magkakaiba. [Ang mga residente ng mga teritoryong may mga hindi bumobotong Delegado o Residenteng Komisyoner ay maaaring magbigay ng pangalan ng Delegado o Komisyoner. Katanggap-tanggap din sa anumang pahayag na ang teritoryo ay walang (bumobotong) mga Kinatawan sa Kongreso.]

Kailangan mong matukoy kung ano ang distrito nakatira ka sa upang kilalanin ang iyong Kinatawan. Kinatawan ay maaaring magbago. / Los representantes están sujetos cambios
Pinagmulan: http://www.house.gov enero 2020

You must determine what district you live in to identify your Representative.

Representatives are subject to change

Source: http://www.house.gov January 2020

See back of the book and write your answer here:

____

24. Who does a U.S. Senator represent?

All people of the state

24. Sino ang kumakatawan ng Senador ng Estados Unidos?

lahat ng mga tao ng estado

25. Why do some states have more Representatives than other states?

There are three correct answers. You need to know one answer.

Because of the state's population

Because they have more people

Because some states have more people

25. Bakit ang ilang estado ay may mas maraming Kinatawan kaysa ibang mga estado?

(dahil sa) populasyon ng estado

(dahil) maraming tao sa kanila

(dahil) mas maraming tao sa ilang estado

26. We elect a President for how many years?

Four (4)

26. Naghahalal tayo ng Pangulo para sa ilang taon?

apat (4)

27. In what month do we vote for President?*

November

27. Sa anong buwan tayo bumoboto para sa Pangulo?*

Nobyembre

28. What is the name of the President of the United States now?*.

Joe Biden

28. Ano ang pangalan ng Pangulo ng Estados Unidos ngayon?*

Joe Biden

Biden

29. What is the name of the Vice President of the United States now?

Kamala Harris.

29. Ano ang pangalan ng Pangalawang Pangulo ng Estados Unidos ngayon?

Kamala Harris.

Harris

30. If the President can no longer serve, who becomes President?

The Vice President

30. Kung ang Pangulo ay hindi na nakakapaglingkod, sino ang nagiging Pangulo?

ang Pangalawang Pangulo

31. If both the President and the Vice President can no longer serve, who becomes President?

The Speaker of the House

31. Kung ang Pangulo at ang Pangalawang Pangulo ay hindi na nakakapaglingkod, sino ang nagiging Pangulo?

ang Ispiker ng Kapulungan

32. Who is the Commander in Chief of the military?

The President

32. Sino ang Punong Kumander ng militar?

ang Pangulo

33. Who signs bills to become laws?

The President

33. Sino ang pumipirma ng mga panukalang-batas upang maging mga batas?

 ang Pangulo

34. Who vetoes bills?

 The President

34. Sino ang nagbebeto sa mga panukalang-batas?

 ang Pangulo

35. What does the President's Cabinet do?

 Advises the President

35. Ano ang ginagawa ng Gabinete ng Pangulo?

 nagpapayo sa Pangulo

36. What are two Cabinet-level positions?

 Secretary of Agriculture

 Secretary of Commerce

 Secretary of Defense

 Secretary of Education

 Secretary of Energy

Secretary of Health and Human Palingkurang

Secretary of Comfort Country (Homeland Security)

Secretary of Housing and City

Secretary of the Interior

Secretary of Labor

Secretary of State

Secretary of Transportation

Secretary of the Treasury

Secretary of Veterans Affairs

Attorney General

Vice President

36. Ano ang dalawang posisyon na nasa antas ng Gabinete?

Kalihim ng Agrikultura

Kalihim ng Komersiyo

Kalihim ng Depensa

Kalihim ng Edukasyon

Kalihim ng Enerhiya

Kalihim ng mga Palingkurang Pangkalusugan at Pantao

Kalihim ng Kapanatagan ng Bansa (Homeland Security)

Kalihim ng Pabahay at Pagpapaunlad ng Lunsod

Kalihim ng Interyor

Kalihim ng Paggawa

Kalihim ng Estado

Kalihim ng Transportasyon

Kalihim ng Tesorerya

Kalihim ng mga Gawain ng mga Beterano

Abugado Heneral

Pangalawang Pangulo

37. What does the judicial branch do?

Reviews laws

Explains laws

Resolves disputes (disagreements)

decides if a law goes against the Constitution

37. Ano ang ginagawa ng sangay na panghukuman?

nirerepaso ang mga batas

ipinaliliwanag ang mga batas

nilulutas ang mga pagtatalo (hindi pagkakasundo)

ipinapasiya kung ang isang batas ay labag sa

Konstitusyon

38. What is the highest court in the United States?

The Supreme Court

38. Ano ang pinakamataas na hukuman sa Estados Unidos?

ang Korte Suprema

39. How many justices are on the Supreme Court?

Nine (9)

39. Ilan ang mga mahistrado sa Korte Supreme?

siyam (9)

40. Who is the Chief Justice of the United States?

John G. Roberts, Jr.

40. Sino ang Punong Mahistrado ng Estados Unidos

ngayon?

John Roberts (John G. Roberts, Jr.)-

41. Under our Constitution, some powers belong to the federal government. What is one power of the federal government?

Know one of the following:

To print money

To declare war

To create an army

To make treaties

41. Sa ilalim ng ating Konstitusyo, ang ilang kapangyarihan ay nasa pederal na pamahalaan. Ano ang isang kapagyarihan ng pederal na pamahalaan?

maglimbag ng pera

magdeklara ng digmaan

bumuo ng isang armi

gumawa ng mga kasunduan

42. Under our Constitution, some powers belong to the states. What is one power of the states?

provide learning and education

provide protection (police)

provide safety (fire departments)

provide a driver's license

to approve zoning and land use

42. Sa ilalim ng ating Konstitusyon, ang ilang kapangyarihan ay nasa mga estado. Ano ang isang

kapangyarihan ng mga estado?

magkaloob ng pag-aaral at edukasyon

magkaloob ng proteksiyon (pulisya)

magkaloob ng kaligtasan (mga kagawaran ng bumbero)

magbigay ng lisensiya para sa pagmamaneho

mag-aproba ng pagsosona at paggamit ng lupa

43. Who is the Governor of your state?

Answers will vary. Residents of the District of Columbia and U.S. territories without a Governor should say "we don't have a Governor."

See back of the book and write your answer here:

____

Governors are subject to change.

Source:

http://en.wikipedia.org/wiki/List_of_current_United_States_g

overnors January 2020

43. Sino ang Gobernador na iyong estado ngayon?

Ang mga sagot ay magkakaiba. [Ang mga residente

ng District of Columbia ay dapat sumagot na ang D.C.

ay

Listahan ng mga Governors ng Estado

Governors ay maaaring magbago.

Pinagmulan:

http://en.wikipedia.org/wiki/List_of_current_Unit

ed_States_governors

44. What is the capital of your state?*

Answers will vary. District of Columbia residents

should answer that D.C. is not a state and does not

have a capital. Residents of U.S. territories should name the capital of the territory.

44. Ano ang kapital ng iyong estado?*

Ang mga sagot ay magkakaiba. [Ang mga residente ng District of Columbia ay dapat sumagot na ang D.C. ay hindi isang estado at walang kapital. Ang mga residente ng mga teritoryo ng Estados Unidos ay dapat sabihin ang kapital ng teritoryo.]

See back of the book and write your answer here:

---

45. What are the two major political parties in the United States?*

Democratic and Republican

45. Ano ang dalawang pangunahing partidong pampulitika sa Estados Unidos?*

Democratic at Republican

46. What is the political party of the President now?

Democraticn Party

46. Ano ang partidong pampulitika ng Pangulo ngayon?

Democratic (Party)

47. What is the name of the Speaker of the House of

Representatives now?

Kevin McCarthy

47. Ano ang pangalan ng Ispiker ng Kapulungan ng mga

Kinatawan?

Kevin McCarthy

Rights and Responsibilities
Mga Karapatan at Responsibilidad

48. There are four amendments to the Constitution about who can vote. Describe one of them.

Citizens eighteen (18) and older can vote.

Any citizen can vote. (Women and men can vote.)

48. May apat na susog sa Konstitusyon tungkol sa kung sino ang makakaboto. Ilarawan ang isa sa mga ito.

Mga mamamayang labingwalong (18) taong gulang at mas matanda (ay makakaboto).

Hindi mo kailangang magbayad (ng isang poll tax) upang makaboto.

Sinumang mamamayan ay makakaboto. (Ang mga babae at mga lalaki ay makakaboto.)

Isang lalaking mamamayan ng anumang lahi (ay makakaboto).

49. What is one responsibility that is only for United States citizens?*

Serve on a jury

49. Ano ang isang responsibilidad na para lamang sa mga mamamayan ng Estados Unidos?*

magsilbi sa isang hurado

bumoto sa isang pederal na halalan

50. What are two rights only for United States citizens?

Apply for a federal job

vote

50. Sabihin ang isang karapatan na para lamang sa mga mamamayan ng Estados Unidos.

bumoto sa isang pederal na halalan

kumandidato para sa pederal na katungkulan

51. What are two rights of everyone living in the United States?

Freedom of expression

Freedom of speech

51. Ano ang dalawang karapatan ng bawat isang naninirahan sa Estados Unidos?

kalayaang magpahayag

kalayaang magsalita

kalayaang magtipun-tipon

kalayaang magpetisyon sa pamahalaan

kalayaang sumamba

karapatang magdala ng armas

52. What do we show loyalty to when we say the Pledge of Allegiance?

The United States and the flag

52. Katapatan sa ano ang ipinapakita kapag sinasabi natin ang Pledge of Allegiance?

sa Estados Unidos

sa bandera

53. What is one promise you make when you become a United States citizen?

Defend the Constitution and laws of the United States

53. Ano ang isang pangako na ginagawa mo kapag ikaw ay naging mamamayan ng Estados Unidos?

isuko ang katapatan sa ibang mga bansa

ipagtanggol ang Konstitusyon at mga batas ng Estados Unidos

sundin ang mga batas ng Estados Unidos

maglingkod sa militar ng Estados Unidos (kung kailangan)

maglingkod (gumawa ng mahalagang trabaho para sa bansa (kung kailangan)

maging matapat sa Estados Unidos

54. How old do citizens have to be to vote?*

Eighteen (18) and older

54. Ilang taon kailangan ang mga mamamayan upang makaboto para sa Pangulo?*

labingwalong (18) taong gulang at mas matanda

55. What are two ways that Americans can participate in their democracy?

vote

join a political party

help with a campaign

join a civic group

join a community group

give an elected official your opinion on an issue

call Senators and Representatives

public support or oppose an issue or policy

run for office

55. Ano ang dalawang paraan na ang mga Amerikano ay maaaring lumahok sa kanilang demokrasya?

bumoto

sumapi sa isang partidong pampulitika

tumulong sa isang kampanya

sumapi sa isang sibikong grupo

sumapi sa isang grupong pangkomunidad

bigyan ang isang inihalal na opisyal ng iyong opinyon sa isang isyu

tawagan ang mga Senador at Kinatawan

pampublikong suportahan o salungatin ang isang isyu o patakaran

kumandidato para sa katungkulan

sumulat sa isang pahayagan

56. When is the last day you can send in federal income tax forms?*

April 15

56. Ano ang huling araw na maaari mong ipadala ang pederal na income tax forms?*

Abril 15

57. When must all men register for the Selective Service?

Between eighteen (18) and twenty-six (26)

57. Kailangan dapat magparehistro ang lahat ng mga lalaki sa Selective Service?

sa edad na labingwalo (18)

sa pagitan ng labingwalo (18) at dalawamp't-anim (26)-

AMERICAN HISTORY

KASAYSAYAN NG AMERIKA

42

Colonial Period and Independence
Panahong Kolonyal at Kalayaan

58. What is one reason colonists came to America?

freedom

political liberty

freedom of religion

economic opportunity

practice their religion

escape persecution58. Ano ang isang dahilan kung

bakit pumunta sa Amerika ang mga colonist?

kalayaan

kalayaang pampulitika

kalayaan sa relihiyon

pagkakataong pangkabuhayan

ipraktis ang kanilang relihiyon

tumakas sa pag-uusig

59. Who lived in America before the Europeans arrived?

    Native Americans

    American Indians

59. Sino ang nanirahan sa Amerika bago dumating ang mga Europeo?

    Mga Amerikanong Indiyan

    Mga Katutubong Amerikano

60. What group of people was taken to America and sold as slaves?

    Africans

60. Anong grupo ng mga tao ang dinala sa Amerika at ipinagbili bilang mga alipin?

    Mga Aprikano

    mga tao mula sa Aprika

61. Why did the colonists fight the British?

    Because of high taxes (taxation without representation)

    Because the British army stayed in their houses (boarding, quartering)

Because they didn't have self-government

61. Bakit nilabanan ng mga colonist ang British?

dahil sa mga matataas na buwis (pagbubuwis nang walang pagkatawan)

dahil ang armi ng British ay tumigil sa kanilang mga bahay (kumakain, naninirahan)

dahil wala silang sariling pamahalaan

62. Who wrote the Declaration of Independence?

Thomas Jefferson

62. Sino ang sumulat ng Deklarasyon ng Kalayaan?

(Thomas) Jefferson

63. When was the Declaration of Independence adopted?

July 4, 1776

63. Kailan ipinagtibay ang Deklarasyon ng Kalayaan?

Hulyo 4, 1776

64. There were 13 original states. Name three.

New Hampshire

Massachusetts

Rhode Island

Connecticut

New York

New Jersey

Pennsylvania

Delaware

Maryland

Virginia

North Carolina

South Carolina Georgia

64. May 13 orihinal na estado. Magsabi ng tatlo.

65. What happened at the Constitutional Convention?

The Constitution was written.

65. Ano ang nangyari sa Kombensiyon para sa

Konstitusyon?

Ang Konstitusyon ay isinulat.

Isinulat ng mga Tagapagtatag na Ama ang

Konstitusyon.

66. When was the Constitution written?

1787

66. Kailan isinulat ang Konstitusyon?

1787

67. The Federalist Papers supported the passage of the U.S. Constitution. Name one of the writers.

James Madison

67. Ang mga Pederalistang Papel ay sumuporta sa pagpasa ng Konstitusyon. Tukuyin ang isa sa mga sumulat.

(James) Madison

(Alexander) Hamilton

(John) Jay

Publius

68. What is one thing Benjamin Franklin is famous for?

U.S. diplomat

68. Ano ang isang bagay na sikat si Benjamin Franklin?

diplomat ng Estados Unidos

pinakamatandang miyembro ng Kombensiyon para

sa Konstitusyon

unang Postmaster General ng Estados Unidos

sumulat ng "Poor Richard's Almanac"

sinimulan ang mga unang libreng aklatan

69. Who is the "Father of Our Country"?

George Washington

69. Sino ang "Ama ng Ating Bansa"?

(George) Washington

70. Who was the first President?*

George Washington

70. Sino ang unang Pangulo?*

George Washington

71. What territory did the United States buy from France in

1803?

The Louisiana Territory

71. Anong teritoryo ang binili ng Estados Unidos mula sa
France noong 1803?

ang Louisiana Territory

Louisiana

72. Name one war fought by the United States in the 1800s..

Spanish-American War

72. Magsabi ng isang digmaan na nakipaglaban ang
Estados Unidos noong mga taon ng 1800.

Digmaan ng 1812

Digmaang Meksikano-Amerikano

Digmaang Sibil

73. Name the U.S. war between the North and the South.

The Civil War

73. Tukuyin ang digmaan ng Estados sa pagitan ng Hilaga
at Timog.

ang Digmaang Sibil

ang Digmaan sa pagitan ng mga Estado

74. Name one problem that led to the Civil War.

Slavery

74. Sabihin ang isang problema na humantong sa Digmaang Sibil.

pang-aalipin

mga dahilang pangkabuhayan

mga karapatan ng estado

75. What was one important thing that Abraham Lincoln did?*

Freed the slaves (Emancipation Proclamation)

75. Ano ang isang mahalagang bagay na ginawa ni Abraham Lincoln?*

pinalaya ang mga alipin (Proklamasyon ng Paglaya)

iniligtas(o pinangalagaan) ang Union

pinamunuan ang Estados Unidos sa Digmaang Sibil

76. What did the Emancipation Proclamation do?

Freed the slaves

76. Ano ang ginawa ng Proklamasyon ng Paglaya?

pinalaya ang mga alipin

pinalaya ang mga alipin sa Confederacy

pinalaya ang mga alipin sa mga estadong

Confederate

pinalaya ang alipin sa karamihan ng mga estado sa

Timog

77. What did Susan B. Anthony do?

Fought for women's rights

77. Ano ang ginawa ni Susan B. Anthony?

nakipaglaban para sa mga karapatan ng mga babae

nakipaglaban para sa mga karapatang sibil

Recent American History

and Other Important Historical Information

Huling Kasaysayan ng Amerika at Ibang Mahalagang

Impormasyong Pangkasaysayan

78. Name one war fought by the United States in the 1900s.*

World War I

World War II

Korean War

War in Vietnam

War (Persian) Gulf

78. Sabihin ang isang digmaan na nakipaglaban ang

Estados Unidos noong 1900s.*

Unang Digmaang Pandaigdig

Ikalawang Digmaang Pandaigdig

Digmaan sa Korea

Digmaan sa Vietnam

Digmaan sa (Persian) Gulf

79. Who was President during World War I?

Woodrow Wilson

79. Sino ang Pangulo noong Unang Digmaang Pandaigdig?

(Woodrow) Wilson

80. Who was President during the Great Depression and World War II?

Franklin Roosevelt

80. Sino ang Pangulo sa panahon ng Great Depression at Ikalawang Digmaang Pandaigdig?

(Franklin) Roosevelt

81. Who did the United States fight in World War II?

Japan, Germany and Italy

81. Sino ang nakalaban ng Estados Unidos noong Ikalawang Digmaang Pandaigdig?

Japan, Germany, at Italy

82. Before he was President, Eisenhower was a general. What war was he in?

World War II

82. Bago siya naging Pangulo, si Eisenhower ay isang heneral. Sa anong digmaan siya nakipaglaban?

Ikalawang Digmaang Pandaigdig

83. During the Cold War, what was the main concern of the United States?.

Communism

83. Sa panahon ng Cold War, ano ang pangunahing inaalala ng Estados Unidos?

Komunismo

84. What movement tried to end racial discrimination?

civil rights movement

84. Anong kilusan ang nagtangkang tapusin ang diskriminasyon sa lahi?

mga karapatang sibil (kilusan)

85. What did Martin Luther King, Jr. do?*

Fought for civil rights

85. Ano ang ginawa ni Martin Luther King, Jr.?*

nakipaglaban para sa mga karapatang sibil

kumilos para sa pagkakapantay-pantay para sa lahat

ng mga Amerikano

86. What major event happened on September 11, 2001 in

the United States?

Terrorists attacked the United States..

86. Anong malaking pangyayari ang nangyari noong

Setyembre 11, 2001, sa Estados Unidos?

Inatake ng mga terorista ang Estados Unidos

87. Name one American Indian tribe in the United States.

Cherokee

Navajo

Apache

[Adjudicators will be supplied with a complete list.].

[Suministrarán una lista completa.]

87. Magsabi ng isang tribo ng Amerikanong Indiyan sa

Estados Unidos.

[Ang mga Opisyal USCIS ay bibigyan ng isang listahan ng mga tribo ng Amerikanong Indiyan na kinikilala ng pederal na pamahalaan.]

Cherokee

Navajo

Sioux

Chippewa

Choctaw

Pueblo

Apache

Iroquois

Creek

Blackfeet

Seminole

Cheyenne

Arawak

Shawnee

Mohegan

Huron

INTEGRATED CIVICS

PINAGSAMANG SIBIKA

Geography

88. Name one of the two longest rivers in the United States.

    Missouri or Mississippi river

88. Magsabi ng isa sa dalawang pinakamahabang ilog sa Estados Unidos.

    Missouri (River)

    Mississippi (River)

89. What ocean is on the West Coast of the United States?

    Pacific Ocean

89. Anong karagatan ang nasa West Coast ng Estados Unidos?

    Pacific (Ocean)

90. What ocean is on the East Coast of the United States?

Atlantic Ocean

90. Anong karagatan ang nasa East Coast ng Estados Unidos?

Atlantic (Ocean)

91. Name one U.S. territory.

Puerto Rico

91. Magsabi ng isang teritoryo ng Estados Unidos.

Puerto Rico

U.S. Virgin Islands

American Samoa

Northern Mariana Islands

Guam

92. Name one state that borders Canada.

New York

92. Magsabi ng isang estado na naghahangga sa Canada.

Maine

New Hampshire

Vermont

New York

Pennsylvania

Ohio

Michigan

Minnesota

North Dakota

Montana

Idaho

Washington

Alaska

93. Name one state that borders Mexico.

California

93. Magsabi ng isang estado na naghahangga sa Mexico.

California

Arizona

New Mexico

Texas

94. What is the capital of the United States?*

Washington, D.C.

94. Ano ang kapital ng Estados Unidos?*

Washington, D.C.

95. Where is the Statue of Liberty?*

New York Harbor

Liberty Island [Also acceptable are New Jersey, near New York City, and on the Hudson (River).]

95. Nasaan ang Istatwa ng Kalayaan?*

New York (Harbor)

Liberty Island [Tinatanggap din ang New Jersey, malapit sa New York City, at nasa Hudson (River).]

Symbols

Mga Simbolo

96. Why does the flag have 13 stripes?

   Because there were 13 original colonies

96. Bakit may 13 guhit ang bandera?

   dahil may 13 orihinal na colony

   dahil ang mga guhit ay kumakatawan sa mga orihinal

   na colony

97. Why does the flag have 50 stars?*

   Because there is one star for each state

97. Bakit may 50 bituin ang bandera?*

   dahil may isang bituin para sa bawat estado

   dahil ang bawat bituin ay kumakatawan sa isang

   estado

   dahil may 50 estado

98. What is the name of the national anthem?

   The Star-Spangled Banner

98. Ano ang tawag sa pambansang awit?

The Star-Spangled Banner

Holidays.

Mga Piyesta Opisyal

99. When do we celebrate Independence Day?*

July 4

99. Kailan tayo nagdiriwang ng Araw ng Kalayaan?*

Hulyo 4-12-

100. Name two national U.S. holidays.

New Year

Martin Luther King, Jr..

Presidents' Day

Memorial Day

Independence Day

Labor Day

Columbus Day

Veterans Day

Thanksgiving Day

Christmas

100. Magsabi ng dalawang pambansang Piyesta Opisyal ng Estados Unidos.

Bagong Taon

Kaarawan ni Martin Luther King, Jr.

Presidents' Day

Memorial Day

Araw ng Kalayaan

Araw ng Manggagawa

Columbus Day

Araw ng mga Beterano

Araw ng Pasasalamat

Pasko

SAMPLE WRITTEN SENTENCES

You will be asked to write a sample sentence. Normally you can make up to three (3) errors in writing and still pass the test.

Be careful to listen to each word the examiner reads. Make sure to write each word, even if you think it is not needed grammatically, if the examiner reads a word; please write out every word that is dictated.

1) A senator is elected for 6 years.

2) Michael Pence is the Vice President of the United States.

3) All people want to be free.

4) America is the land of freedom.

5) All American citizens have the right to vote.

6) America is the home of the brave.

7) America is the land of the free.

8) Joe Biden is the President of the United States.

9) Citizens have the right to vote.

10) Congress is part of the American government.

11) Congress meets in Washington DC.

12) Congress passes laws in the United States.

13) George Washington was the first president.

14) I want to be a citizen of the United States.

15) I want to be an American citizen.

16) I want to become an American so I can vote.

17) It is important for all citizens to vote.

18) Many people come to America for freedom.

19) Many people have died for freedom.

20) Martha Washington was the first lady.

21) Only Congress can declare war.

22) Our Government is divided into three branches.

23) People in America have the right to freedom.

24) People vote for the President in November.

25) The American flag has stars and stripes.

26) The American flag has 13 stripes.

27) The capital of the United States is Washington DC.

28) The colors of the flag are red white and blue.

29) The Constitution is the supreme law of our land.

30) The flag of the United States has 50 stars.

31) The House and Senate are parts of Congress

32) The President enforces the laws.

33) The President has the power of veto.

34) The President is elected every 4 years.

35) The President lives in the White House.

36) The President lives in Washington D.C.

37) The President must be an American citizen.

38) The President must be born in the United States.

39) The President signs bills into law.

40) The stars of the American flag are white.

41) The White House is in Washington, DC.

42) The United States flag is red white and blue.

43) The United States of America has 50 states.

Members of the Senate

Senators of the 118th Congress

Representatives are subject to change.

Find your state to identify your two Senators

Source: http://Senate.gov Updated January 2020

What is a class? - Article I, section 3 of the Constitution requires the Senate to be divided into three classes for purposes of elections. Senators are elected to six-year terms, and every two years the members of one class—approximately one-third of the senators—face election or reelection. Terms for senators in Class I expire in 2020, Class II in 2021, and Class III in 2023.

U.S. State Postal Abbreviations List

Alabama – AL   Alaska – AK   Arizona – AZ   Arkansas - AR

California – CA   Colorado – CO   Connecticut - CT

Delaware – DE   District of Columbia - DC

Florida - FL

Georgia - GA

Hawaii - HI

Idaho – ID   Illinois – IL   Indiana – IN   Iowa - IA

Kansas – KS   Kentucky - KY

Louisiana - LA

Maine – ME   Maryland – MD   Massachusetts – MA

Michigan – MI   Minnesota – MN   Mississippi – MS

Missouri – MO   Montana - MT

Nebraska – NE   Nevada – NV   New Hampshire – NH

New Jersey – NJ   New Mexico – NM   New York – NY

North Carolina – NC   North Dakota - ND

Ohio – OH   Oklahoma – OK   Oregon - OR

Pennsylvania - PA

Rhode Island - RI

South Carolina – SC   South Dakota - SD

Tennessee – TN   Texas - TX

Utah - UT

Vermont – VT   Virginia - VA

Washington – WA   West Virginia – WV   Wisconsin – WI
Wyoming - WY

US Commonwealth and Territories

American Samoa – AS   Federated States of Micronesia – FM
Guam – GU   Marshall Islands - MH

Northern Mariana Islands – MP   Palau – PW   Puerto Rico –
PR   Virgin Islands

Senators of the 118th Congress

Senators of the 118th Congress

Source:
https://en.wikipedia.org/wiki/118th_United_States_Congress*=

Class - Article I, section 3 of the Constitution requires the Senate
to be divided into three classes for purposes of elections.
Senators are elected to six-year terms, and every two years the
members of one class—approximately one-third of the senators—
face election or reelection.

Tommy Tuberville   Republican   Alabama

Katie Britt   Republican   Alabama

Lisa Murkowski   Republican   Alaska

Dan Sullivan Republican   Alaska

Kyrsten Sinema   Democratic   Arizona

Mark Kelly   Democratic   Arizona

John Boozman   Republican   Arkansas

Tom Cotton   Republican   Arkansas

Dianne Feinstein Democratic   California

Alex Padilla   Democratic   California

Michael Bennet   Democratic   Colorado

John Hickenlooper   Democratic   Colorado

Richard Blumenthal   Democratic   Connecticut

Chris Murphy   Democratic Connecticut

Tom Carper Democratic Delaware

Chris Coons Democratic Delaware

Marco Rubio Republican Florida

Rick Scott   Republican Florida

Jon Ossoff Democratic Georgia

Brian Schatz Democratic Hawaii

Mazie Hirono   Democratic Hawaii

Mike Crapo Republican Idaho

Jim Risch   Republican Idaho

Dick Durbin Democratic Illinois

Tammy Duckworth   Democratic Illinois

Todd Young Republican Indiana

Mike Braun Republican Indiana

Chuck Grassley Republican Iowa

Joni Ernst   Republican Iowa

Jerry Moran Republican Kansas

Roger Marshall Republican Kansas

Mitch McConnell Republican Kentucky

Rand Paul   Republican Kentucky

Bill Cassidy Republican Louisiana

John Neely Kennedy Republican Louisiana

Susan Collins   Republican Maine

Angus King Independent Maine

Ben Cardin Democratic Maryland

Chris Van Hollen Democratic   Maryland

Elizabeth Warren Democratic   Massachusetts

Ed Markey   Democratic   Massachusetts

Debbie Stabenow   Democratic   Michigan

Gary Peters Democratic   Michigan

Amy Klobuchar   Democratic   Minnesota

Tina Smith   Democratic   Minnesota

Roger Wicker   Republican   Mississippi

Cindy Hyde-Smith   Republican   Mississippi

Josh Hawley Republican   Missouri

Eric Schmitt Republican   Missouri

Jon Tester   Democratic   Montana

Steve Daines   Republican   Montana

Deb Fischer Republican   Nebraska

Ben Sasse   Republican   Nebraska

TBD   Republican   Nebraska

Catherine Cortez Masto   Democratic   Nevada

Jacky Rosen Democratic   Nevada

Jeanne Shaheen Democratic   New Hampshire

Maggie Hassan   Democratic   New Hampshire

Bob Menendez   Democratic   New Jersey

Cory Booker Democratic   New Jersey

Martin Heinrich   Democratic   New Mexico

Ben Ray Luján   Democratic   New Mexico

Chuck Schumer   Democratic   New York

Kirsten Gillibrand Democratic   New York

Thom Tillis   Republican   North Carolina

Ted Budd   Republican   North Carolina

John Hoeven   Republican   North Dakota

Kevin Cramer   Republican   North Dakota

Sherrod Brown   Democratic   Ohio

J. D. Vance   Republican   Ohio

James Lankford   Republican   Oklahoma

Markwayne Mullin   Republican   Oklahoma

Ron Wyden   Democratic   Oregon

Jeff Merkley   Democratic   Oregon

Bob Casey, Jr.   Democratic   Pennsylvania

John Fetterman   Democratic   Pennsylvania

Jack Reed   Democratic   Rhode Island

Sheldon Whitehouse   Democratic   Rhode Island

Lindsey Graham   Republican   South Carolina

Tim Scott   Republican   South Carolina

John Thune   Republican   South Dakota

Mike Rounds Republican   South Dakota

Marsha Blackburn   Republican   Tennessee

Bill Hagerty   Republican   Tennessee

John Cornyn Republican   Texas

Ted Cruz   Republican   Texas

Mike Lee   Republican   Utah

Mitt Romney Republican   Utah

Bernie Sanders   Independent Vermont

Peter Welch *   Democratic   Vermont

Mark WarnerDemocratic   Virginia

Tim Kaine   Democratic   Virginia

Patty Murray Democratic   Washington

Maria Cantwell   Democratic   Washington

Joe Manchin Democratic   West Virginia

Shelley Moore Capito Republican   West Virginia

Ron Johnson   Republican   Wisconsin

Tammy Baldwin   Democratic   Wisconsin

John Barrasso   Republican   Wyoming

Cynthia Lummis Republican   Wyoming

List of State Governors

Governors are subject to change. District of Columbia residents should answer that D.C. is not a state and does not have a capital. Residents of U.S. territories should name the capital of the territory.

Source:
https://en.wikipedia.org/wiki/List_of_current_United_States_gover nors

*Denotes newly elected Governors

Alabama – Kay Ivey

Alaska – Mike Dunaway

Arizona – To be determined

Arkansas – Asa Hutchinson.

California – Gavin Newsom

Colorado – Jared Polis

Connecticut – Ned Lamont

Delaware – John Carney

Florida – Ron DeSantis

Georgia – Brian Kemp

Hawaii – David Ige

Idaho – Brad Little

Illinois – J.B. Pritzker

Indiana – Eric Holcomb

Iowa – Kim Reynolds

Kansas – Laura Kelly

Kentucky – Andy Beshear

Louisiana – John Bel Edwards

Maine – Janet Mills

Maryland – Larry Hogan

Massachusetts – Charlie Baker

Michigan – Gretchen Whitmer

Minnesota – Tim Walz

Mississippi – Tate Reeves

Missouri – Mike Parson

Montana – Greg Gianforte*

Nebraska – Jim Pillen

Nevada – Steve Sisolak

New Hampshire – Chris Sununu

New Jersey – Phil Murphy

New Mexico – Michelle Lujan Grisham

New York – Kathy Hochul

North Carolina – Ray Cooper

North Dakota – Doug Burgum

Ohio – Mike DeWine

Oklahoma – Kevin Stitt

Oregon – Tina Kotek

Pennsylvania – Josh Shapiro

Rhode Island – Daniel McKee

South Carolina – Henri McMaster

South Dakota – Kristi Noem

Tennessee – Bill Lee

Texas – Greg Abbott

Utah – Spencer Cox

Vermont – Phil Scott

Virginia – Glenn Youngkin

Washington – Jay Inslee

West Virginia – Jim Justice

Wisconsin – Tony Evers

Wyoming – Mark Gordon

List of State Capitols

Alabama - Montgomery

Alaska - Juneau

Arizona - Phoenix

Arkansas - Little Rock

California - Sacramento

Colorado - Denver

Connecticut - Hartford

Delaware - Dover

Florida - Tallahassee

Georgia - Atlanta

Hawaii - Honolulu

Idaho - Boise

Illinois - Springfield

Indiana - Indianapolis

Iowa - Des Moines

Kansas - Topeka

Kentucky - Frankfort

Louisiana - Baton Rouge

Maine - Augusta

Maryland - Annapolis

Massachusetts - Boston

Michigan - Lansing

Minnesota - St. Paul

Mississippi - Jackson

Missouri - Jefferson City

Montana - Helena

Nebraska - Lincoln

Nevada - Carson City

New Hampshire - Concord

New Jersey - Trenton

New Mexico - Santa Fe

New York - Albany

North Carolina - Raleigh

North Dakota - Bismarck

Ohio - Columbus

Oklahoma - Oklahoma City

Oregon - Salem

Pennsylvania - Harrisburg

Rhode Island - Providence

South Carolina - Columbia

South Dakota - Pierre

Tennessee - Nashville

Texas - Austin

Utah - Salt Lake City

Vermont - Montpelier

Virginia - Richmond

Washington - Olympia

West Virginia - Charleston

Wisconsin - Madison

Wyoming – Cheyenne

ABOUT THE AUTHOR

77

Mike Swedenberg saw a need to assemble a study guide to help those persons wishing to immigrate to the United States whose second language is English. This study guide is annotated with the names of current Representatives that all applicants must know. The list is current for State Governors, US Senators and US Congressmen. This list will be updated at each election cycle.

Other books by the Author

A New York Wedding – a novel

Bully Boss – a novel

The Road Warrior a sales manual

Advertising Copywriting and the Unique Selling Proposition

Smart Money Stupid Money

21 ½ Things to Know Before Self-Publishing

How to Publish an eBook

How to Publish a Book in Print

The Short Stories by Mike Swedenberg